THEN & NOW

MONTGOMERY

THEN & NOW

MONTGOMERY

Carole A. King and Karren Pell

We dedicate this book to Jeff Benton. Jeff's excellent research and productivity have blazed a trail for those seeking to learn about Montgomery's architectural history. He has been our gracious and generous benefactor—always willing to share work and knowledge. In this book, we leaned heavily on Jeff's work, and we honor him as a scholar, a preservationist, a gentleman, and friend.

Published by Arcadia Publishing
Charleston, South Carolina

Printed in the United States of America

For all general information, please contact Arcadia Publishing:
Telephone 843-853-2070
Fax 843-853-0044
E-mail sales@arcadiapublishing.com
For customer service and orders:
Toll-Free 1-888-313-2665

Visit us on the Internet at www.arcadiapublishing.com

ON THE FRONT COVER: At the downtown end of Commerce Street, Hebe, from her view at the top of the fountain, gazes toward the eternal flow of the Alabama River. As the goddess of youth and cupbearer to the Olympic gods, Hebe symbolizes Montgomery's pride and faith in its past, present, and future. (Courtesy of Algernon Blair-Landmarks Foundation Collection; Timothy Henderson.)

ON THE BACK COVER: This 1934 photograph shows construction workers celebrating the completion of the Veterans Hospital on Perry Hill Road. Algernon Blair was the contractor for the hospital. The hospital continues to serve those who have served their country. (Courtesy of Algernon Blair Collection- Montgomery County Historical Society.)

CONTENTS

ACKNOWLEDGMENTS

The first groups we wish to thank are those responsible for the fact that many of Montgomery's historic buildings are able to be "Now" photographs: Landmarks Foundation of Montgomery, Montgomery County Historical Society (MCHS), and the Alabama Historical Commission. James Loeb pioneered the historic preservation movement in Montgomery. His efforts to preserve Montgomery's rich architectural heritage are visible, in part, as the "Now" photographs. The dedication, tireless vigilance, and work in preservation of the following individuals also stand out: Mary Ann Neeley, James Fuller, Jeff Benton, and Robert Gamble. These organizations and individuals continue to lead the Montgomery preservation movement. We credit Mary Ann Neeley's and Jeff Benton's research as the main source of our information. Finding the majority of the information for this book did not require us to dig and search, as these scholars had blazed a wide, clear trail, and we were lucky and honored to follow it. We also appreciate Mary Ann for digging through her files for photographs, answering our phone calls, and sharing her wealth of information. We also owe a debt of gratitude to James Fuller for helping us find photographs in the MCHS collection. Although Tommy Oliver is no longer with us, his gracious love of "place" and the research he left behind continue to inspire us. Bob McLain at Old Alabama Town was most helpful, and we thank him. Other sources for information and photographs deserving acknowledgment include the Historic American Building Survey (HABS) and the Alabama Departments of Archives and History (ADAH). We especially thank Meredith McLemore of ADAH. We thank Jeff Feet for his essential contribution to the "Now" photographs. We appreciate Steve Jones, the director of emergency management for the City of Montgomery, for giving us roof access for some great pictures; also, our thanks go to Officer Milton Burkette for being our guide. Another note concerning "Now" photographs—we acknowledge Russell Stringer, Montgomery's urban forester, and his tree planting program. His leafy success made our job of taking "Now" photographs difficult, but we are thankful for the trees! Carole King took the majority of the "Now" photographs, but Tim Henderson also took pictures, gave technical support, and fixed us great food so we didn't faint or breakdown at the computer; his contributions are most appreciated. We thank our editor, Brinkley Taliaferro, for guidance and patience.

INTRODUCTION

One way to view Montgomery's changes from the past to the present is to see events, people, and locations as connected. For example, the trolley line, the "Lightning Route," in Montgomery, Alabama, was among the first public trolley systems in North America. The trolley was the most influential factor in developing neighborhoods and parks beyond the city limits. The neighborhoods it fostered were also among the first developments in the South that came to be known as suburbs. A specific location can own a similar effect. On the day of Confederate president Jefferson Davis's inauguration, a parade marched up Dexter Avenue to the capitol. More recent history recognizes the importance of Dr. Martin Luther King's march from Selma that also culminated at the capitol on Dexter Avenue.

Such recognition of the need for a connection to the past is a large element of the historic preservation movement. In Montgomery, the Landmarks Foundation is credited with saving and encouraging the preservation of many historic structures. Downtown, the antebellum Winter Building, which stands at Court Square, was renovated by the law firm of Balch and Bingham. In April 1861, Montgomery was the capital of the Confederacy. From the Winter Building's second story, Gen. Leroy Pope Walker, secretary of war for the Confederate States of America, sent General Beauregard the telegram to fire on Fort Sumter. Constructed by a founding family and standing in the heart of the city since 1841, the Winter Building has witnessed the rise and fall of the Confederacy, the celebration of the end of two World Wars, and the marches of the civil rights period. The Winter Building currently awaits its incarnation as part of the current downtown Montgomery renovation project "City of Dreams."

Before the trolley provided service beyond the city limits, most residents lived in close proximity to the downtown area. Although those neighborhoods are now gone, many individual structures remain in place and some have been moved to other sites. John Poston Figh, a prominent Montgomery contractor, originally built the townhouse of Albert Pickett in 1837. In 1858, Figh sold the house to Albert James Pickett, Alabama's first historian. Pickett died before moving into the house, but his widow, Sarah Smith Harris Pickett, lived there until 1894. The house has a colorful history, as it hosted many famous guests (including Confederate president Jefferson Davis), was commandeered by Union troops during Montgomery's occupation by Wilson's Raiders at the end of the Civil War, and became the location for the beloved Barnes School for Boys. In June 1996, the large home was moved to South Court Street to make way for the expansion of the Federal Building. Today, the townhome of Alabama's first historian is loved, used, and appreciated as the headquarters of the Montgomery County Historical Society.

Neighborhoods developed beyond the city limits, promising clean air and country living. Capitol Heights, Old Cloverdale, and the Garden District remain popular residential areas today, as the homes and communities offer the ambience of another time combined with comfort and convenience important to modern life. The Garden District claims one of the most famous residences, the Alabama Governor's Mansion. Built in 1907 by the adjutant general of Alabama, Robert Fulwood Ligon Jr., the house has been the residence of Alabama's chief executive since 1951. A series of renovations and updates has made the house more comfortable and functional as the governor's residence, but the house's current facade remains very close to its original.

Parks have always been popular with the people of Montgomery. Early on, residents enjoyed the quiet, cool shade offered by the many old oak trees that gave Oakwood Cemetery its name. Although the gazebo that accommodated visitors in the late 1800s to the early 1900s is gone, many people still enjoy walking, and even running, along the historic cemetery's paths. Later, parks outside the city limits became popular. A sad part of Montgomery's history came to pass when city leaders closed all parks rather than integrate them according to the US Supreme Court ruling in 1959. The large iron gates of Oak Park, near Montgomery's first suburban neighborhood, Highland Park, were locked. Today, the gates of Oak Park have been swung open, and Montgomery residents of all ethnicities enjoy picnics, strolls along shady paths, or a bit of solitude on a garden bench.

From Montgomery's founding, schools and churches have filled an important role. Sidney Lanier High School, Montgomery's first coeducational high school, celebrates the 100th anniversary of its founding in 2011. The school's original location was at the corner of South McDonough and Scott Streets. That building currently serves as the Baldwin Arts and Academic Magnet Public School. In 1929, a new building was constructed for Lanier, south of downtown on South Court Street. The school remains an active and beloved neighborhood school. Historic St. John's Episcopal Church has stood on Madison Avenue since the mid-1800s. Confederate president Jefferson Davis and his family worshiped there, and his pew is still marked. The famous Dexter Avenue King Memorial Baptist Church, where Dr. Martin Luther King was pastor, also still proudly stands and hosts pilgrims from around the world.

So, it is that avenues, buildings, houses, and parks hold on to Montgomery's history and serve as landmarks for the present and guideposts into the future. Therefore, it serves all of Montgomery's citizens here in the present to look closely at the places of the past and to hear and to feel the whispers and feelings of then and now.

CHAPTER 1

BUSINESS AS USUAL

Montgomery was founded on the Alabama River. Early on, riverboats were the chief means of transportation; later, the railroads laid tracks along the riverbed. This 1907 photograph shows a riverboat resting against a sand bar, a train rumbling along the tracks, and a background full of factories. The factories are now gone, and the riverboats no longer ply the river as a main means of commerce, but freight trains still rumble beside the beautiful Alabama River. (Courtesy of Art Work Collection.)

In 1886, the *Alabama* was loaded with cotton and other goods at the dock in downtown Montgomery. The city depended on steamboats to provide both commercial and personal transportation. Today, the *Harriett II*, a modified steamboat, also works hard, but its objective is the relaxation and entertainment of her passengers. (Courtesy of MCHS.)

A busy Dexter Avenue was a sign of the times in 1907. Almost all businesses, wholesale and retail, were located downtown. Originally named Market Street, Dexter Avenue was Montgomery's main street. From the 1950s, the downtown area became quiet. Today, the signs of change appear as large facades announce the upcoming renovation of Dexter Avenue as part of Montgomery's "City of Dreams" project. (Courtesy of Art Work Collection.)

In 1927, the Kress Store burned. In 1929, the building that replaced it collapsed. The third, and current, building's design, which borrows elements from the Temple of Hera, was inspired when Samuel Kress was knighted by the king of Italy for helping preserve ancient monuments. Kress closed in 1981, but the building stayed open as a variety store until 1997. Today, it plays a leading role in the "City of Dreams" renovation phase. (Courtesy of Landmarks Foundation Collection.)

In 1891, J.N. Curbow and A.L. Clapp built a retail store for their monument business on upper Dexter Avenue. The company's fine work has stood the test of time and can be seen today in homes, tombstones, and the Confederate Memorial on the Alabama State Capitol grounds.

Pictured from left to right are (in the windows) A.P. Wilson and George Townsend; (on the ground) J.N. Curbow and A.L. Clapp. Public parking now occupies the site. (Courtesy of ADAH-Landmarks Foundation Collection.)

For the comfort of its passengers arriving in Montgomery on over 40 trains a day, the Louisville and Nashville (L&N) Railroad built the handsome redbrick Union Station and the 600-foot shed in 1898 at Water Street. Passenger trains stopped coming through Montgomery in 1979, but freight trains still rumble by and whistle. Union Station remains a busy destination because it houses the Montgomery Welcome Center and the ever-popular Thai restaurant with the clever name Railroad Thai. (Courtesy of Landmarks Foundation Collection.)

The office for Western Union Telegraph stood at 40 1/2 Commerce Street. This 1913 photograph of the deliverymen on bicycles shows both the importance of the telegram regarding communication and also the close proximity of downtown businesses. The building is privately owned and undergoing restoration as part of the "City of Dreams" project. (Courtesy of ADAH-Landmarks Foundation Collection.)

This 1950s photograph shows the second block of Dexter Avenue between North Perry and North Lawrence Streets. The Alabama Power Company later moved down Dexter Avenue to the antebellum Montgomery Advertiser Building, and Sears, Roebuck and Company moved out of downtown to one of the first "big box" stores on South Court Street. The building was demolished, and currently the site serves as parking for Retirement Systems of Alabama (RSA) tower. (Courtesy of Collier-Landmarks Foundation Collection.)

Todd's Gun Store, with its suspended, oversized rifle, was long a landmark in downtown Montgomery. This 1950 photograph shows it at its location facing North Court Street. Later, it moved farther down North Court Street. The site is now occupied by an office building and parking. (Courtesy of Collier-Landmarks Foundation Collection.)

Burke's Drugstore wrapped around the street corner at North Court and Monroe Streets, causing the location to be known as "Burke's corner." On Saturdays, when townspeople and folks from the country congregated, the street was full of shoppers. The building was lost to urban renewal efforts and replaced with a glass office building. Times continue to change, and the office building is currently undergoing renovations to be converted into lofts. (Courtesy of Holloway-Landmarks Foundation Collection.)

The Cathcart-Rogers Furniture Company stood on Monroe Street; the ornamental dome made it easy to recognize. Not visible in this photograph, Montgomery City Hall stood to its right. When city hall burned, the Cathcart-Rogers Building, along with the other structures in this photograph, survived. In a 1937 photograph of the new city hall, the Cathcart dome is visible; however, it did not survive the relentless push of progress, and a parking deck now stands in its place. (Courtesy of Collier-Landmarks Foundation Collection.)

The Jefferson Davis Hotel was built in 1927. In the 1930s, WSFA radio station operated out of one of the top floors. Singer Hank Williams was a regular guest on the radio's musical program. Although the hotel remained segregated into the 1960s, Rev. Ralph Abernathy and Martin Luther King Jr. were allowed to broadcast sermons on Sundays. The hotel has been converted into apartments and is considered a valuable part of the on-going Montgomery Street renovations. (Courtesy of Landmarks Foundation Collection.)

In this c. 1950 photograph of the south side of Monroe Street, the old Montgomery Theatre is in the foreground. Built in 1860, the theater hosted many famous actors and even the infamous John Wilkes Booth. The theater closed in 1907 and housed Webber's Department Store for many years. It is currently vacant and awaiting a new role as a prominent actor in Montgomery's "City of Dreams." (Courtesy of Collier-Landmarks Foundation Collection.)

Looking down Lee Street at the intersection of Montgomery Street, farmers and merchants gather at cotton warehouses to bargain and buy. Today, Troy University, the Davis Theatre, and the Rosa Parks Library Museum are transforming the intersection from business to a cultural and educational center. (Courtesy of Art Work Collection.)

North Side, First Block of Washington Avenue

In 1902, the H.F. Copeland Stables stood on the north side, the first block, of Washington Avenue. In an interesting association, a parking deck for municipal employees working in the Montgomery City Hall Annex currently stands in its place. (Courtesy of Copeland-Landmarks Foundation Collection.)

George Manegold's father founded the candy-manufacturing business on Commerce Street in 1870. After the building burned in 1912, Manegold became one of the many businesses moving from the center of town to Madison Avenue. Selling both candy and tobacco, the store reopened in 1913. The area had been a well-respected residential development, and in this photograph the Winter-Freeman house, designed by noted architect Samuel Sloan, is still standing. The Manegold Building now serves as the Montgomery Fire Department Headquarters. (Courtesy of ADAH-Landmarks Foundation Collection.)

Although the trolleys made living outside the city limits feasible, by the 1950s the private automobile was the main mode of transportation. Cars needed gas, and therefore gas stations became fixtures in Montgomery's first suburbs.

This c. 1955 photograph shows a classic Gulf station on Fairview Avenue and Cleveland Avenue (now Rosa Parks Avenue). The gas station has been replaced by a CVS drugstore. (Courtesy of Landmarks Foundation Collection.)

A note on the back of this 1940s photograph, identifies the people standing in front of the service station as, from left to right, John Walker, Maggie Morgan, J.W., and Thomas; the last names of J.W. and Thomas, as well as any names for the other four workers, are missing. Today, the building is used for storage and parking. Note the remains of the Dr. Pepper advertisement painted on the brick wall behind the service station. (Courtesy of MCHS.)

CHAPTER 2

HEBE'S COURT

At one end of Dexter Avenue, the capitol presides; at the other end, Hebe, topping the fountain, holds court. On January 15, 1923, the inaugural parade of Gov. W.W. "Plain Bill" Brandon traveled from Court Square up Dexter Avenue. Dexter Avenue was decorated with banners and flags, and Hebe, the fountain's crowning goddess, ruled over all. (Courtesy of Landmarks Foundation Collection.)

In 1894, this block of retail buildings stood at the end of Court Square. In the 1960s, these buildings were lost to urban renewal. A new building, One Court Square, took its place as the function of downtown had changed—the shopping mall replaced downtown, and downtown needed office and parking space. Today, One Court Square, renamed Dexter Plaza, will soon assume its new life as the downtown library and children's museum. (Courtesy of Art Work Collection.)

The Winter Building was erected in 1840 for a branch of the St. Mary's Bank. The Magnetic Telegraph Company occupied an upper floor. From the Winter Building, the Confederate government sent the telegram to fire on Fort Sumter—the action that started the Civil War. As the war continued, telegraph operators read casualty lists to people waiting in the square below. Today, people wait for another kind of news—who will be the new resident of the Winter Building. (Courtesy of HABS-Landmarks Foundation Collection.)

Court Square got its name from the first courthouse of the new Alabama territory that stood close by. Although all court business moved to a new courthouse in 1894, the name remained. In the 1880s, banking and retail reigned, along with Hebe. In 1888, the Moses Brothers Banking and Realty Company, then Montgomery's largest business, built the city's first six-story "skyscraper" on Court Square. In 1907, the Moses Building was torn down to construct the First National Bank, which is currently vacant. (Courtesy of Art Work Collection.)

Shown here in a 1917 photograph, the First National Bank Building originally featured a row of lions' heads. Later, the bank became First Alabama Bank, and during a mid-1970s exterior renovation, the lions' heads were removed and a dark "bonnet" banded around the building's top. However, four of the lions were mounted on steles, where they remain close to the new roundabout at Court Square as a reminder of the past and a pleasant feature of the present. (Courtesy of Library of Congress-Landmarks Foundation Collection.)

In the mid-1850s, the Klein Building was erected as the location for the Central Bank of Alabama. Bank owner William Knox hired architect Stephen Decatur Button, who also designed Montgomery's first capitol and Knox's home. The bank financially supported the Confederacy and, after the war, closed its doors. In the 1920s, Klein and Sons retail store acquired the building. The Klein Building is currently empty and awaiting a new life. (Courtesy of ADAH-Landmarks Foundation Collection.)

The original Exchange Hotel, built in 1846, was the political and social center of Montgomery. It served as office space for the early Confederate government and as temporary residence for Confederate president Jefferson Davis and his wife, Varina. In 1905, the old Exchange was demolished and a new one built (pictured). It was also popular until the 1970s, when downtown's life started to wane. It was demolished in 1974. Then, in 1996, the Colonial Company constructed a modern building on the site. (Courtesy of Landmarks Foundation Collection.)

Decorating the fountain has long been a tradition. On May 12, 1919, the fountain was draped in red, white, and blue to welcome the 167th Rainbow Division returning from World War I. In April 2011, the Joy to Life Foundation "pinked" the fountain to raise awareness of breast cancer and to promote its annual walk/run. (Courtesy of ADAH-Landmarks Foundation Collection.)

HEBE'S COURT

FOR THE PEOPLE

Trolleys provided transportation to downtown and beyond the city limits. This trolley waits in front of the capitol to take passengers to Pickett Springs Park. Andrew Dexter, one of Montgomery's founders, donated the elevated site, informally known as Goat Hill, at the end of Dexter Avenue for a capitol. The avenue is named for him—the hill for his goats. (Frazier family collection.)

Montgomery's first capitol burned in 1849; the current one was built in 1850–1851. In 1861, Confederate president Jefferson Davis took the oath of office on the steps of the capitol, and a brass star marks the spot where he stood. In March 1965, the Selma-to-Montgomery civil rights march, led by Dr. Martin Luther King, ended at the capitol steps. The capitol and grounds remain a gathering place for tourists and residents alike, who enjoy its beauty and history. (Courtesy of Art Work Collection.)

The Corinthian capitals of the capitol's portico were based on designs originating from Athens's Tower of the Winds (c. 40 BCE); the Renaissance Revival–style dome was perhaps based on the dome of St. Paul's Cathedral in London (1700). In 1885, the east wing was added, and by 1912 both the north and south wings were constructed following designs by Montgomery's premier architect, Frank Lockwood. The capitol of Alabama—the pride of all its citizens—shines in the sun by day and is lit by night. (Courtesy Algernon Blair-MCHS.)

The first courthouse on this site was built in 1854. In 1894, the front steps of the 1854 building were removed, and a center section and the west wing were added. Most of the 1854 building remained as the east wing of the 1894 courthouse. In 1956, the joint building of 1854 and 1894 was demolished, and the current county courthouse was erected on the same spot at Washington Avenue and South Lawrence Street. (Courtesy of Art Work Collection.)

The Scott Street Firehouse, built before 1898, is the oldest surviving firehouse in Montgomery and remained in service as such until 1966. The building originally housed horses and fire engines and provided dormitory-like accommodations for firemen. Until 1898, the city only had a volunteer fire department. The last horses that hauled fire engines, Joe and Ed, were retired in 1926. The firehouse was renovated in 1980 to accommodate business offices. The building is now for sale. (Courtesy of Art Work Collection.)

In 1894, the police station stood on the north side of city hall and the market (1871), which burned in March 1932. After the fire, the new city hall, which was neo-Georgian in architectural style, was designed by Frank Lockwood Jr., built by Algernon Blair, and financed by the city and the Works Progress Administration. The city hall was dedicated on September 30, 1937. Hank Williams's funeral was held in the building's auditorium. City hall is currently undergoing renovations. (Courtesy of ADAH-Landmarks Foundation Collection.)

The Federal Courthouse and Post Office Building opened in 1884 on Dexter Avenue and South Lawrence Street. Montgomery was proud of the building, not only for its grandeur, but because its foundation was made of Alabama stone, and the building boasted Montgomery's first elevator. Compass Bank now occupies the site. (Courtesy of McClurkin-Landmarks Foundation Collection.)

The Scottish Rite Masonic Temple on Dexter Avenue was built in 1926 and featured an Egyptian motif. The building, remodeled in 1938 in a Neo-Classical design for the home of the Alabama Supreme Court, became known as the Judicial Building. The building became vacant in 1993, and in 2007 preservationists thwarted developers wanting to demolish the historic building for parking. Currently, the old Judicial Building is undergoing another change—a new RSA (Retirement Systems Alabama) building is being constructed around it. (ADAH.)

FOR THE PEOPLE

The Dorsey Cottage, now located at Old Alabama Town, is typical of the cottages that were popular in Montgomery during the mid-1850s. The Southern Poverty Law Center, at the Dorsey Cottage's original site, is an internationally known organization that is dedicated to fighting hate and bigotry and to seeking justice for the most vulnerable members of society. (Courtesy of Landmarks Foundation Collection.)

The Seibels-Ball-Lanier house was built in 1855; John Jacob Seibels bought the home in 1858. When demolished in 1988, the last of Montgomery's high-style antebellum Italianate homes was lost. Close the site stands the Civil Rights Memorial Center, an interactive museum focused both on the civil rights movement and teaching tolerance. (Courtesy of Art Work Collection.)

CHAPTER 4

MIND, BODY, AND SPIRIT

Cottage Hill School, the namesake of the Cottage Hill neighborhood, opened in April 1891 and burned in 1904. This image is part of a series of 1894 photographs of important places in Montgomery. (Courtesy of Art Work Collection.)

Herron Street School, at 2001 Herron Street, was included in the 1907 series of photographs of important Montgomery landmarks. At the time of this image, Virginia Hereford was principal. This building was assembled from the remains of the previous school building, known as Cottage Hill School. Currently, the Hatton Brown Publishing Company is housed behind a small rise on the site. (Courtesy of Art Work Collection.)

The Perley Gerald House was built around 1851 on the southeast corner of South Lawrence and Adams Streets. The Sisters of Loretta purchased and used the house as a convent from 1873 to 1962. Next to the house, in 1890, the sisters constructed a Victorian building, called the Annex, for classroom space for its school, St. Mary's of Loretta Academy. The entire block is now the site of the Montgomery County Courthouse and the Phelps-Price Justice Center. (Courtesy of James Bozeman.)

St. John's, the oldest Episcopal parish in Montgomery, was organized in 1834. In 1855, the church (pictured) was designed by the nation's foremost church architects, Wills and Dudley of New York, and built facing Madison Avenue. Confederate president Jefferson Davis and his wife, Varina, attended services at St. John's; their pew is still marked. The most recent addition in 2009 was painstakingly designed to match the original facade. (Courtesy of Art Work Collection.)

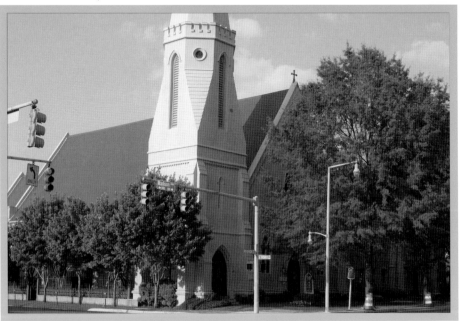

MIND, BODY, AND SPIRIT

The cornerstone of the Dexter Avenue Methodist Church was laid in 1892; it took several years to finish the building. The decorative brickwork is credited to J.B. Worthington, who is also known for the work on Sayre Street School. The stonework was done by Montgomery's Curbow and Clapp Marble Company. Exterior and interior renovations have taken place, but the church is easily recognizable. The church has stood the test of time, and so has its congregation— many of the current members are descendants of the church's early members. (Courtesy of Art Work Collection.)

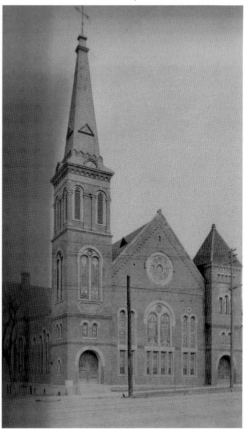

The congregation of First
Baptist Church on North Ripley
Street formed in 1867; the
Romanesque Revival–style brick
building was finished about
1915. Its nickname, "Brick-a-
Day Church," refers to African
American members contributing
a brick each day to complete the
building. During the civil rights
movement, Ralph Abernathy was
pastor. The church was active in
the Bus Boycott and the Freedom
Ride on May 20, 1961. Freedom
Riders met at the church on May
21, which was then attacked by
a white mob. Today, the church
and its members stand as a
testament to faith and freedom.
(Courtesy of Landmarks
Foundation Collection.)

Started in 1905, the construction of First Baptist Church on South Perry Street was not finished until 1923, as the work was completed only as the congregation could pay. This was done so that the church did not incur debt. Architect George Norrman of Atlanta based the church's design on Brunelleschi's famous cathedral built in Florence in the 1400s. The distinguishing feature of the church is its huge dome covered in red tiles. (Courtesy of Art Work Collection.)

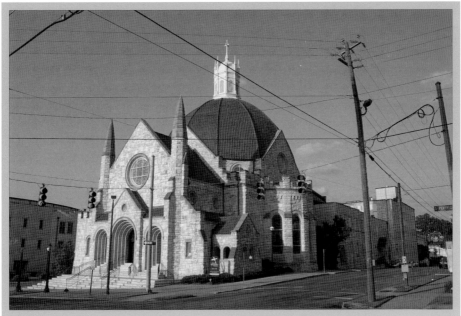

The Dexter Avenue King Memorial Baptist Church was built in the 1880s on the former site of a slave trader's pen. Dr. Martin Luther King Jr. was pastor here from 1954 to 1960. In March 1960, the congregation left the church expecting to see other African American congregations joining them to march peaceably; however, white police officers blocked the march. Today, the church remains home to an active congregation and is a popular and beloved civil rights landmark. (Courtesy of Nelson Malden-ADAH.)

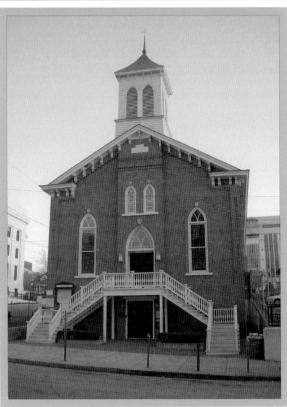

Temple Beth Or was built in 1901 on the southwest corner of Clayton and Sayre Streets after outgrowing its first place of worship constructed in 1862. When the congregation erected a new Beth Or on Narrow Lane Road in 1958, they moved the stained-glass windows from the 1901 building and installed them in the new structure. After the building's demolition, Joe Scott Motor Company, established in 1946, moved to the Clayton Street location. Note the fun Scottie flags. (Courtesy of Art Work Collection.)

Oakwood Cemetery, Montgomery's oldest burial ground, began as land donated by Andrew Dexter and John Scott and was known as "Scott's Free Burying Ground." Although the first recorded burial was in 1818, tradition holds that internments began in 1810; thus, the centennial was celebrated in 1910 by building the ornamental gateway. During the early 1900s, the cemetery was used often as a park. Today, runners, walkers, and those seeking solitude still enjoy its beauty and quiet. (Courtesy of Art Work Collection.)

In 1920, the Fresh Air Camp provided cottages and health care for tuberculosis patients. Since antibiotics were not available until 1946, patients suffering from the deadly and contagious disease were quarantined in sanatoriums or camps. A prevailing belief that fresh air had curative value encouraged camps, such as this one on a hill on Upper Wetumpka Road that was maintained by the Anti-Tuberculosis League. Eventually, a permanent tuberculosis sanatorium was built. Currently, Greil Memorial Psychiatric Hospital stands on the site. (Courtesy of Landmarks Foundation Collection.)

In 1898, Reverend Murphy, rector of St. John's Church, was instrumental in securing a grant from Andrew Carnegie to build a free, public library. The cornerstone for the library, built in the Beaux-Arts Classicism style, was laid in 1902. Opening in 1904, it was the first free public library in Alabama. The Juliette Morgan Library became the main library in the early 1960s. The Carnegie Library Building is currently used by the Montgomery County Appraisal Department. (Courtesy of Art Work Collection.)

Sayre Street School, the oldest public school building in Montgomery, was built in 1891. Its most distinguished design element is J.B. Worthington's brickwork. Shown in this May 1926 photograph are students at Sayre Street School who performed *The Winds* at the Spirit of the South Pageant. The pageant was part of Montgomery's observance of Alabama Homecoming Week, a statewide celebration. The school closed in 1976. Since 1997, the building has housed Jean & Co., a florist. (Courtesy of MCHS.)

MIND, BODY, AND SPIRIT

St. Margaret's Hospital, run by the Roman Catholic Sisters of Charity, was built around the 1900s on land once owned by Governor Watts; his home was used as a chapel and housing for the sisters and other nurses. The hospital's pebbledash building had a red tile roof and stood facing Adams Street. St. Margaret's Hospital also served as a training school for nurses. By the 1920s, it was Montgomery's largest hospital. Today, the site is occupied by state agencies. (Courtesy of Art Work Collection.)

This 1907 photograph shows the girls' high school, also known as Central High School, at the corner of Lawrence and High Streets. Young women attended high school in this building from 1894 to 1910. The structure also served as an elementary school until 1924, and then it housed the Montgomery Museum until it was demolished in 1959. The main city library, the Juliette Hampton Morgan Memorial Library, now occupies the site. (Courtesy of Art Work Collection.)

1A26

Sidney Lanier High School is named for a Southern poet who lived in Montgomery following the Civil War. The consolidated high school, designed by Frederick Ausfield and built by Algernon Blair, opened in September 1929 and is still open. Late-Gothic architectural decorations, including stone shields, open books, and lamps of knowledge, make a distinguished statement about the importance of education. (Courtesy of James Bozeman.)

MIND, BODY, AND SPIRIT

HOME, SWEET HOME

In the early 1900s, due to the trolley making commuting feasible, beautiful homes were built on the outskirts of Montgomery along Perry Street. When the residential area that included Perry Street sought historic designation, it was named the Garden District. Many historic homes on Perry Street were lost to the interstate. However, Perry Street remains an impressive thoroughfare, lined by trees and stately historic homes. (Courtesy of Landmarks Foundation Collection.)

The Branch-Ray Mansion at 730 South Court Street is shown here in the 1920s while it was still the Branch family home. On the front walk stands Edward J. Branch (left) and William Thomas Branch. Later, the house became the American Legion headquarters and part of the HABS survey in 1934. The beautiful home was lost to the interstate. (Courtesy of Anne Tidmore.)

The Figh-Pickett House, the oldest surviving brick residence in Montgomery, was built about 1837 by John Figh on 14 Clayton Street. In 1858, Albert James Pickett, Alabama's first historian, bought the house. During Montgomery's occupation, Union officers commandeered the house. From 1907 to 1942, the house was the Barnes School for Boys. In 1996, the Montgomery County Historical Society acquired the house for its headquarters and moved the building to 512 South Court Street. (Courtesy of HABS-Landmarks Foundation Collection.)

Built in the 1830s, the First White House of the Confederacy stood at the corner of Bibb and Lee Streets. When Montgomery became the Confederate capital, Pres. Jefferson Davis and his wife, Varina, lived in the house. Currently, the site boasts one of the first constructions of the downtown renovation project, which is a skateboard park where the younger set enjoys the sport. The house is now a museum and is located next to the Alabama Department of Archives and History. (Courtesy of Art Work Collection.)

Berry Owen, a prosperous livery stable operator, built his home in 1848 on 468 South Perry Street. In 1852, he sold his house and his business and left Montgomery. On April 12, 1865, Union troops occupied the house. William Martin Teague and his wife, Eugenia Isabelle Jackson, bought the home in 1889. The house is one of Montgomery's finest examples of the Greek Revival style. Since 1993, it has been the home of the Alabama Historical Commission. (Courtesy of Art Work Collection.)

The Murphy House was built by John Murphy in 1851. In April 1865, the home was used as the Union Army provost marshal's headquarters during the occupation of Montgomery during the Civil War. The house served as the Elks Lodge from 1894 to 1970. The house currently is the office of the Montgomery Water Works and Sanitary Sewer Board—a connection to John Murphy, who was director of the Montgomery Water Works in 1854. (Courtesy of Art Work Collection.)

The Lomax House, at 221 South Court Street, may have been built as early as 1845. Gen. Tennent Lomax and his wife, Caroline Billingslea, moved into the house in 1857. General Lomax died in the Battle of Seven Pines, and Caroline Lomax remained at the residence until her death in 1907. Memories remain of the many events, social and political, that were hosted in the home through those years. The home currently houses law offices. (Courtesy of Art Work Collection.)

In 1848, William Knox, a banker and Confederate supporter, commissioned Stephen Decatur Button, the architect who designed Montgomery's capitol, to design Knox Hall. Knox lived in the house until he died in 1869; his wife, Anna Lewis Knox, lived in the house until she died in 1890. From 1902 to 1907, the house was the Beauvoir Club. In the 1920s, its conversion to an apartment house included a four-story addition that hid the mansion. When the apartment complex was demolished, the old mansion was rediscovered and restored. It currently houses commercial property. (Courtesy of Art Work Collection.)

New research indicates that the McBryde-Screws-Tyson House may have its core beginning in 1838 when Dr. Andrew McBryde and his wife, Ann, first built on Mildred Street. By 1854, the home was finished in a Greek Revival style. Ann McBryde sold the home to *Montgomery Advertiser* editor William Screws in 1885. In 1890, Screws sold the home to John Tyson, a politician and planter. Fred and Dianne Bush, known for their restorations of homes in Cottage Hill, currently own the home. (Courtesy of HABS and Fred Bush.)

The Brittan-Dennis House was built in the 1850s by newspaperman Patrick Brittan. Described as Montgomery's finest remaining brick cottage, it retains its colonnaded porch, paired cornice brackets, and etched ruby glass sidelights and transom. It sits on its original site, restored and managed by Landmarks as leased property connected to Old Alabama Town. (Courtesy of Landmarks Foundation Collection.)

Robert Howlett built his family home on the northeast corner of North McDonough and Columbus Streets in the early 1850s. He died in the yellow fever epidemic of 1854. In this 1900s photograph, from left to right, stand Mary Elizabeth Howlett Scott, Annie Julia Howlett, and unidentified children and boarders. The house was demolished, and the offices of Old Alabama Town occupy the site today. (Courtesy of Landmarks Foundation Collection.)

A note on the back of this 1905 picture calls it "the old home at 3 Whitman Street." The note lists the women's first names, but only one of their individual identities is certain. Recent research reveals that "Mama," on the steps in the dark shawl, is Milwood Pruitt Barry; the other women are Mary Ernest Barry Lamont, Rebecca Barry, and Arlene Barry. The house later became the kitchen/den area of the large house at 508 Clayton, which is still standing. (Courtesy Landmarks Foundation Collection.)

Forbes Liddell constructed this impressive home on Highland Avenue around 1900. He was a successful wholesale electrical and mill supply dealer downtown. The house was later moved around the corner to Forest Avenue. The home is now Odessa's Blessing, a catering service featuring traditional Southern cuisine. (Courtesy of Art Work Collection.)

This house was built at the corner of Adams and Union Streets in 1858 by lawyer Jefferson Franklin Jackson, who later sold it to Charles Molton. By the early 1880s, it was known as the Woman's Home. A 1920 publication explained that it provided "shelter for widows, orphans, and old maiden ladies." Landmarks Foundation moved and restored it at Old Alabama Town. The Retirement Systems of Alabama Headquarters was built on the site in 2009. (Courtesy of Art Work Collection.)

In 1894, Joseph Kennedy finished the Victorian Queen Ann mansion, known as the Kennedy-Sims House, at 556 South Perry Street. Kennedy designed the house; tradition holds that its many ornamental details were the result of his childhood dreams. The unique, ornate interior rivals the detail of the exterior. In 1980, William Newell saved the home and restored it. It is currently a commercial property. (Courtesy of Art Work Collection.)

The Sabel-Cantey House, Montgomery's only example of the Chateauesque style, was built at 644 South Perry Street in 1903. Samuel Sabel was a merchant; Sabel Steel is currently managed by the fifth generation of the Sabels. T. Weatherly Carter, who designed the Ligon House, which now serves as the Alabama Governor's Mansion, designed the home. The Sabel-Cantey House is currently a commercial property. (Courtesy of Art Work Collection.)

This postcard shows a view of Perry Street featuring the Ligon Mansion, which now serves as the Alabama Governor's Mansion, and, next to it, the Hill House. The Friends of the Governor's Mansion purchased the Hill House and gave it to the State of Alabama. The Hill House has been restored and is part of the Alabama Governor's Mansion Complex. (Courtesy of James Bozeman.)

Fine Residence Section, Perry Street, Montgomery, Ala

Robert Fulton Ligon Jr. commissioned Montgomery architects T. Weatherly Carter and Benjamin Smith to build his family home at 1142 South Perry Street in 1907. The Ligon family remained until 1951, when Emily Ligon sold it to the State of Alabama (following her mother's wishes) for the governor's mansion. Some elements have been changed to make the home functional for the governor and his family, but the house remains as originally designed. (Courtesy of James Bozeman.)

M-6 Governor's Mansion
Montgomery, Alabama

The Ordeman House was built on North Hull Street in the early 1850s by Charles Ordeman, an architect and investor. Ordeman suffered business losses, and the house was sold at auction in 1854. Julius Caesar Bonaparte Mitchell later acquired the home as his townhouse; he owned a plantation in Mount Meigs. In 1905, the Shaw family acquired the property and eventually sold it to the Landmarks Foundation for restoration. The Ordeman House stands on its original site as a part of Old Alabama Town. (Courtesy of Landmarks Foundation Collections.)

Thomas M. Cowles - Goldthwaite - River Sts 1844

The Cowles House stood on Goldthwaite and River Streets. River, which no longer exists, ran between Bell Street and the Alabama River. Built around 1844, the house later became the office of Alabama Midland Railroad Company by 1894. The house was demolished around 1915. Today, the Hampstead Institute manages a three-acre urban farm that is a part of Community Supported Agriculture and therefore offers instruction on organic and urban gardening on-site. (Courtesy of MCHS.)

CHAPTER 6

FUN AND FROLIC

Pickett Springs was located on the old plantation of Albert Pickett, Alabama's first historian. Called the "the best public resort" by the *Montgomery Advertiser* in 1886, it was four miles north of the city limits in an area now known as Chisholm. Most people took public transportation to the wooded area to enjoy a day of leisure and fresh air. (Courtesy of Art Work Collection.)

Freeney's Tavern, built in 1824, provided a place for travelers to sleep as well as to enjoy libations. It proudly hosted the grand ball given in honor of the Marquis de Lafayette during his 1825 visit. For generations, ladies told of the French hero dancing with their mothers and grandmothers. The building burned in 1926. The Renaissance Hotel presently occupies the site. The Freeney's bell is honored and preserved in the hotel's bar, named Freeney's Bell Tavern. (Courtesy of Art Work Collection.)

Local lore holds that the Freeney's Tavern bell rang at 5:00 p.m. every evening to announce both the end of the working day and time to have a libation at Freeney's Bell Tavern. The original bell is preserved in the Renaissance Hotel bar; a new bell stands beside the lounge's enticing patio. (Courtesy of Tim Henderson.)

The Oak Park Pavilion hosted the dances where the belles of Montgomery and the soldiers from Camp Sheridan met at the start of World War I. Oak Park not only adjoined the Highland Park neighborhood but also featured a pool, a zoo, walking trails, and gardens. Montgomery photographer Stanley Paulger took this photograph of John Mapes (left) and a friend enjoying the pavilion, which is now gone. The current granite block structure houses Montgomery Leisure Services Department. (Courtesy of Gorrie Family-Landmarks Foundation Collection.)

FUN AND FROLIC

The local utility company developed Electric Park to encourage the public to ride the electric trolley. The park, located on Three Mile Branch, was on Line Creek Road, which is now known as Atlanta Highway. The park included rides and a lake large enough for small craft. The electricity to operate lights and rides was produced on-site and further promoted electrical power. The area is now the Forest Hills Shopping Center. (Courtesy of Art Work Collection.)

For decades after the Civil War, a group of women known as The Ladies Memorial Association collected private funds for a Confederate monument. Jefferson Davis laid the cornerstone on May 29, 1886; the dedication ceremony for the finished monument was December 12, 1898. Designed by Alexander Doyle, it stands on the grounds of the Alabama Capitol. It has recently undergone conservation efforts to remediate a century of environmental damage. (Courtesy of Art Work Collection.)

In this c. 1950 photograph, the renowned marching band of Alabama State University passes the Paramount Theatre on Montgomery Street. As noted on the marquee, the building was condemned. Today, named the Davis Theatre in honor of Tine Davis's efforts to save and renovate the building, it is the home of the Montgomery Symphony and the centerpiece of the block's rebirth as a cultural center. The theater is administrated by Troy University. (Courtesy of Collier-Landmarks Foundation Collection.)

The statue of Robert E. Lee originally stood on North Madison Terrace to mark the new residential area, Lee Place. This photograph is from the program of the unveiling ceremony held on June 12, 1908. Later, the statue was moved to Madison Avenue, where it shared duty with a monument to Jefferson Davis welcoming visitors to Montgomery, the first capital of the Confederacy. Currently, the statue stands in front of Robert E. Lee High School on Ann Street. (Courtesy of Landmarks Foundation Collection.)

In this postcard, Col. J.S. Pinkard's home, Rockhaven, the Van Pelt home, and trolley tracks are visible on Madison Avenue. Rockhaven burned in the late 1960s, and the lot stood vacant for several decades. Then, in the late 1980s, the city bought the lot and created a park. The park is named in honor of Louis Armstrong, a local well-loved minister. (Courtesy of James Bozeman.)

Capitol Heights, Montgomery, Ala.

The Great Western Railway freight terminal, built in 1898, is the only one that remains in Montgomery. Its no-nonsense design contrasts sharply with the ornate design of the Union Station passenger depot built about the same time. In 2004, the terminal was renamed Riverwalk Stadium and modified to welcome and seat up to 7,000 fans of the new baseball team, the Montgomery Biscuits. (Courtesy of Montgomery Museum of Fine Arts.)

The first Montgomery Country Club was built in 1903 close by Carter Hill Road. On February 15, 1925, the building burned. In her book *Save Me the Waltz*, Zelda Fitzgerald claimed the cause of the fire was "the fiery explosion of a gallon of moonshine stored in a locker." The current Montgomery Country Club is located at the end of Fairview Avenue. The beautiful building stands regally at the end of an impressive entry drive. (Courtesy of Landmarks Foundation Collection.)

Everybody who enjoys eating and having fun at Sinclair's Restaurant, on the corner of Boultier and Fairview Avenues in the historic neighborhood of Old Cloverdale, can look at the photographs on the wall and learn it used to be a filling station. Its neighbor, the Capri Theatre, has remained popular, and an evening out might combine dinner on the patio at Sinclair's and a movie at the Capri Theatre. (Courtesy of Sinclair's Restaurant.)

FUN AND FROLIC

In 1898, a cotton bale represented many long, hot hours of work. However, these belles have only playful antics on their minds as they pose with a cotton bale for a photographer in a lighthearted moment. Having a fun time seems to have transcended decades as these modern belles, from left to right Jane Coker, Carol Mosley, Carole King, and Karren Pell, toast the Montgomery "City of Dreams" project. (Courtesy of Davidson/Freeborn-Landmarks Foundation Collection and Kelsey Sullivan Payne.)

www.arcadiapublishing.com

Discover books about the town where you grew up, the cities where your friends and families live, the town where your parents met, or even that retirement spot you've been dreaming about. Our Web site provides history lovers with exclusive deals, advanced notification about new titles, e-mail alerts of author events, and much more.

MADE IN THE USA

Arcadia Publishing, the leading local history publisher in the United States, is committed to making history accessible and meaningful through publishing books that celebrate and preserve the heritage of America's people and places. Consistent with our mission to preserve history on a local level, this book was printed in South Carolina on American-made paper and manufactured entirely in the United States.

This book carries the accredited Forest Stewardship Council (FSC) label and is printed on 100 percent FSC-certified paper. Products carrying the FSC label are independently certified to assure consumers that they come from forests that are managed to meet the social, economic, and ecological needs of present and future generations.

FSC
Mixed Sources
Product group from well-managed
forests and other controlled sources

Cert no. SW-COC-001530
www.fsc.org
© 1996 Forest Stewardship Council

Find Your Place in History.